police dogs

1. How many police dogs can you see?
2. Can you see five policemen?
3. Are the police dogs big dogs?
4. How many dogs are running?
5. Can you see a white dog?
6. How many dogs are on leads?
7. What colour is the dog running after the man?
8. Have police dogs ever been to your school?
9. Do you think the man with the gun is a policeman?
10. Do you think the bang from the gun will make the dog run away?

1 Can you see the sun today?
2 What colour is the sun?

3 Can you see the sky today?
4 What colour is the sky?

5 Can you see clouds in the sky?
6 What colour are clouds?

7 Did you put on a coat today?
8 What colour is your coat?

9 Do you have on a jumper today?
10 What colour is your jumper?

11 Have you looked at your reading book today?
12 What colour is your reading book?

1	How many cars can you see?
2	What number is the red car?
3	Is the green car number four?
4	What number is the yellow car?
5	How many boys are in the blue car?
6	Is the black car number six?
7	What number is the white car?
8	How many cars have no one in them?
9	How many girls are in the red car?
10	Do you like riding in bumper cars?
11	How many adults can you see?
12	How many adults are in the cars?

policeman book jumper sun

1 I am soft.
You put me on.
I keep you warm.
I am a —.

2 You can feel me on your skin.
I am far away.
I am hot.
I am the —.

3 You are looking at me now.
I have pages.
You can read me.
I am a —.

4 I have two legs.
I have a dog to help me.
I lock up bad people.
I am a —.

men on the moon

1 Is the moon far away?
2 Can we go to the moon?
3 How many men can you see on the moon?
4 Have children been to the moon yet?
5 Is there much to see on the moon?
6 Do men stay on the moon for a long time?
7 Is it very hot on the moon?
8 Do you think we will all go to the moon one day?

1 How many parcels can you see?
2 Who is the red parcel for?
3 What do you think is in the green parcel?
4 Who is the yellow parcel for?
5 How many blue parcels can you see?
6 Who is the big blue parcel for?
7 Which parcel has pink ribbon round it?
8 Who is the little blue parcel for?
9 Is the red parcel as big as the purple parcel?
10 Who is the green parcel for?

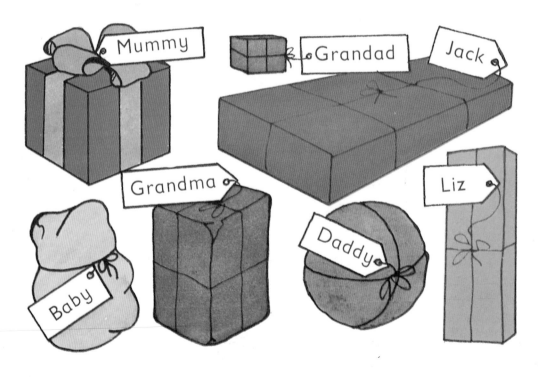

parcels

1. What colour is the cat?
2. Are the kittens the same colour as the cat?
3. Are all the kittens in the basket?
4. How many kittens can you see?
5. What colour is the basket?
6. Are all the kittens asleep?
7. How many kittens are not in the basket?
8. Do you like kittens?
9. How many legs does a cat have?
10. How many tails can you see?
11. Do you have a kitten at home?
12. Do you think it is fun to play with a kitten?

Hey Diddle Diddle
The cat and the fiddle,
The cow jumped over the moon.
The little dog laughed
To see such fun
And the dish ran away with the spoon.

1 Who had a fiddle?
2 Who jumped over the moon?
3 Who laughed?
4 What did the dish run away with?
5 Was the dog a big dog?
6 How many animals are in the poem?
7 Can a real cow jump over the moon?
8 Did this poem make you laugh?

1 How many helicopters can you see?
2 What colour is the helicopter in the middle?
3 Can helicopters fly as fast as jets?
4 Do helicopters have wings?
5 Have you been in a helicopter?
6 Is the green helicopter in front of the blue helicopter?
7 Is one helicopter landing?
8 Do helicopters need to land on a long runway?
9 What colour is the helicopter at the back?
10 Can you see a man hanging from a helicopter?

back   middle   front

helicopter   kitten   parcel   moon

1   I am not very big.
    I am fun to play with.
    I have four legs.
    I am a —.

2   You see me at night.
    I am far away.
    Men can land on me,
    I am the —.

3   I can be big or small.
    I have things in me.
    I have ribbon round me.
    I am a —.

4   You can ride in me.
    I go up in the air.
    I do not need much room to land.
    I am a —.

the boating pond

1   How many boats can you see?
2   What colour is boat number four?
3   Have you been in a boat?
4   How many children are in the red boat?
5   What colour is boat number three?
6   How many boats are empty?
7   How many adults are in the green boat?
8   Do you like being in a boat?
9   Is the red boat full?
10 How many children are in the yellow boat?
11 How much is it to go in a boat?
12 Is there a boating pond near your home?

yes or no

1 Is your teacher a man?
2 Are you a girl?
3 Is it raining outside?
4 Are you happy today?
5 Do you like coming to school?
6 Do you have a pencil in your hand?
7 Is your best friend sitting next to you?
8 Did you clean your teeth today?
9 Do you have a pet in your classroom?
10 Are you seven years old?
11 Is a boy sitting just in front of you?
12 Is a girl sitting on your left?

toy shop

1 What kind of shop is this?
2 How many people are in the shop?
3 What is the man holding in his hand?
4 Can you see a teddy bear?
5 Do you think this shop sells many dolls?
6 What is the boy looking at?
7 What is the girl holding in her hands?
8 What is next to the teddy bear?
9 How many toy cars can you see?
10 Do you like going into toy shops?

1 Are all the donkeys the same colour?
2 How many donkeys can you see?
3 How many children are riding on the donkeys?
4 How many donkeys are standing still?
5 What colour is the man's hat?
6 Have you had a ride on a donkey?
7 Are donkeys as big as horses?
8 Do you think donkeys like being on the sands?
9 Can you see a donkey with a hat?
10 If you had a donkey what would you call it?

donkeys

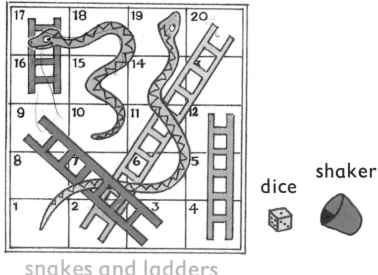

dice

shaker

snakes and ladders

1 Which number is at the top of the red ladder?
2 How many snakes can you see?
3 Which number is at the top of the green ladder?
4 Can you see a blue snake?
5 Which number is at the bottom of the blue ladder?
6 What colour is the longest snake?
7 Which number is at the bottom of the yellow ladder?
8 Do you know how to play snakes and ladders?
9 How many dice can you see?
10 What colour is the shaker?

ladder

dice

donkey

boat

1 You can ride on me.
   I have four legs.
   I say hee haw.
   I am a —.

2 You can ride on me.
   I can be big or small.
   I sail on water.
   I am a —.

3 You can stand on me.
   You can go up and down me.
   I have rungs.
   I am a —.

4 I have numbers on me.
   I have six sides.
   You shake me.
   I am a —.